20th Century
PERSPECTIVES

Key Battles of World War I

David Taylor

Heinemann Library
Chicago, Illinois

© 2001 Reed Educational & Professional Publishing
Published by Heinemann Library,
an imprint of Reed Educational & Professional Publishing,
Chicago, Illinois
Customer Service 888-454-2279
Visit our website at www.heinemannlibrary.com

Designed by AMR
Illustrated by Art Construction and David Cuzik
Originated by Dot Gradations
Printed by Wing King Tong in Hong Kong

05 04 03 02 01
10 9 8 7 6 5 4 3 2 1

Library of Congress Cataloging-in-Publication Data
Taylor, David.
    Key battles of World War I / David Taylor.
        p. cm. -- (20th century perspectives)
    Includes bibliographical references and index.
    ISBN 1-57572-437-5 (library binding)
    1. World War, 1914-1918--Campaigns--Juvenile
    literature. [1. World War, 1914-1918--Campaigns.]
    I. Titles. II. Series.

D521 .T36 2001
940.54'1--dc21
                                        00-063454

Acknowledgments
The author and publishers are grateful to the following for permission to reproduce copyright material: Corbis, pp. 24, 25, 40, 43; Hulton Getty, pp. 23, 27, 37; Imperial War Museum, pp. 10, 11, 13, 15, 16, 17, 19, 20, 21, 29, 31, 32, 34, 39; John Frost, p. 42; Peter Newark, p. 18; The Art Archive, pp. 5, 36; unknown, p. 41.

Cover photograph reproduced with permission of Corbis.

Every effort has been made to contact copyright holders of any material reproduced in this book. Any omissions will be rectified in subsequent printings if notice is given to the publisher.

Some words are shown in bold, **like this.** You can find out what they mean by looking in the glossary.

Contents

War Clouds Gather

Before 1914, there was great rivalry between the **great powers** of Europe. This rivalry resulted in the outbreak of World War I in August 1914. Most people thought that it would be all over by Christmas. How wrong they were! The war lasted for four long years. More than eight million soldiers were killed and more than twenty million more were wounded and disabled.

France and Germany

In 1870–1871, Germany defeated France in the Franco-Prussian War. The Germans took over the French provinces of Alsace and Lorraine. The French wanted their land back and thirsted for revenge.

Britain and Germany

Germany had grown into a powerful country with a large army. It was also busy building its navy and winning an overseas **empire.** All of this worried the British. Britain had the largest empire in the world and its navy had ruled the oceans for a hundred years. It did not like being challenged by Germany. The leaders of the two countries became distrustful of each other.

This map shows Europe in January 1914.

Key
- Triple Entente (The Allies)
- Triple Alliance (Central Powers)

Turkey joined the Central Powers in October 1914. Italy joined the Allies in 1915.

Russia and Austria-Hungary

Austria-Hungary had a large empire in central Europe. It wanted to take over land in an area in southeast Europe known as the **Balkans.** In 1908, Austria–Hungary took control of the small Balkan country of Bosnia. The biggest Balkan country, Serbia, did not like this and wanted to drive the Austrians out. Russia was also interested in the Balkans. It wanted to have access from the Black Sea to the Mediterranean Sea through the Straits of Dardanelles. Russia supported Serbia against the Austrians, but the Austrians had the backing of Germany. It was a tense situation.

The alliance system

The mistrust and suspicion between the great powers led them to group themselves into two **alliances.** Germany, Austria–Hungary, and Italy formed the Triple Alliance. This was rivaled by the Triple Entente—*entente* is French for "agreement"—made up of Britain, France, and Russia. If two countries from the rival alliances went to war, the other four countries would be involved in one way or another. Europe was living on edge.

A fateful day

On June 28, 1914, Archduke Franz Ferdinand, the heir to the Austrian throne, and his wife Sophie were on an official state visit to Sarajevo, the capital city of Bosnia. While driving through the streets, the archduke and his wife were shot dead by Gavrilo Princip, a young Serbian student. The Austrians blamed Serbia for the shootings and this set off a chain reaction of events that, by early August, had plunged Europe into World War I.

A costly wrong turn

The chauffeur of Archduke Franz Ferdinand's car was named Leopold Lojka. As he drove from Sarajevo station to the town hall, Lojka noticed a member of the crowd about to throw a **grenade** at the car. He immediately accelerated, causing the grenade to land on the rolled-up hood of the car, rather than inside it. The grenade fell to the ground. Lojka's quick thinking saved the life of the archduke, who was left shocked and angry.

When they reached the town hall, the archduke decided to leave Sarajevo as quickly as possible. A new route back to the station was quickly planned, but no one told Lojka! As the procession of cars drove off, Lojka turned right off Franz Joseph Avenue instead of going straight. He went to turn around, but could not find reverse gear. Princip seized the moment, ran from the crowd, and shot the archduke in the neck. Sophie, who was pregnant, was shot in the stomach.

The Battle of the Marne, September 5–10, 1914

The outbreak of war was greeted with joy and enthusiasm by many people on all sides. From all over the British **Empire,** men volunteered to fight. They came from Australia, New Zealand, South Africa, Canada, India, and the West Indies. It was thought that the war would be over by the end of the year, but it continued until 1918, mainly because the Germans lost the Battle of the Marne.

The Schlieffen Plan

A German general, Count Alfred von Schlieffen, had made up a plan to knock France out of the war within six weeks. This was to avoid having to fight a war on two fronts. German troops would march through Belgium into northern France and encircle Paris. Once France was beaten, German troops would be sent to fight Russia in eastern Europe.

To begin with, things went well for the Germans. Powerful guns destroyed Belgian forts and allowed the German **infantry** and **cavalry** to advance rapidly. The Belgians fought heroically, but were no match for the might of the German army.

On August 22, 1914, the British Expeditionary Force (BEF), an army of 100,000 men, arrived at Mons in Belgium. Here, the BEF managed to delay the German army, but was then forced to retreat.

This battle map details the Schlieffen Plan and the Battle of the Marne, 1914.

Key

➤ Intended route of German army under the Schlieffen Plan
➤ Actual route of German army
▰▰▰ Bristish and French armies
⚔ Battle of the Marne
⌇ Line of trenches [the Western Front] dug after the Battle of the Marne

The Battle of the Marne, September 5–9, 1914

The German army had been covering up to 31 mi. (50 km) a day and was becoming tired. It had also lost around 100,000 men, who had been sent to fight the Russians on the Eastern Front. So, General von Kluck decided to change the Schlieffen Plan. Instead of sweeping westward around Paris, he ordered the German army to swing to the east.

The British and French gathered their forces together along the Marne River, and decided to make a stand against the Germans. More than 4,000 French reinforcements were rushed to the battlefield from Paris. The battle lasted for five days and ended with the exhausted Germans being pushed back 37 mi. (60 km) to the Aisne River. The **Allies** called their victory "the miracle of the Marne." Paris had been saved from capture, and German hopes of beating France quickly lay in ruins.

Stalemate

The Battle of the Marne was a turning point. Up to now the war had been one of movement. But both sides realized that their modern guns were so accurate and powerful that they would have to dig in and fight a defensive war. It was impossible for infantry and cavalry to move across the open countryside without being shot. Both sides dug a line of trenches from the English Channel to the Swiss border called the **Western Front.** The war became a stalemate—neither side could move.

These British troops are under fire during the Battle of the Marne. One soldier has been shot, and another soldier runs for cover.

War breaks out–how did people react?

The atmosphere was electric, almost unbelievable. We were all excited about it and ready to join in.

Norman Tennant of the British Royal Field Artillery

In Australia at that time we were part of the British Empire and very loyal to Britain. We thought it was our war.

Edward Smout, Australian Medical Corps

We believed that the French army would perform miracles. We did not think for one moment that the war would go on so long or would be so cruel.

Hermine Venot-Focke, French civilian, 1914

Everyone was waving flags. We threw flowers to the marching soldiers. Everyone was singing, "We'll meet again in the Fatherland."

Margarethe Stahl, German civilian, 1914

Trench Systems and Warfare

The trench systems built along the **Western Front** were very complex. The British frontline trenches were between seven and ten feet (two and three meters) deep and five feet (one and a half meters) wide. Either wood or **corrugated** iron strengthened the sides. Huge rolls of barbed wire up to 33 yds. (30 m) wide protected them. Behind the frontline trench were support and communication trenches, along which supplies and troops were moved. The support trenches had **latrines,** kitchens, and supply areas. Behind the trench system were artillery posts, ammunition dumps, and field hospitals.

The German trenches were much deeper than the British ones. Some of them were as deep as 49 ft. (15 m), with underground rooms for the sick and sleeping quarters for the troops. They often had electric lights, piped water, and good ventilation.

This diagram shows a typical trench system on the Western Front.

The area between the two lines of trenches was known as **no-man's-land.** It was usually about 547 yds. (500 m) wide, but sometimes was as narrow as 55 yds. (50 m).

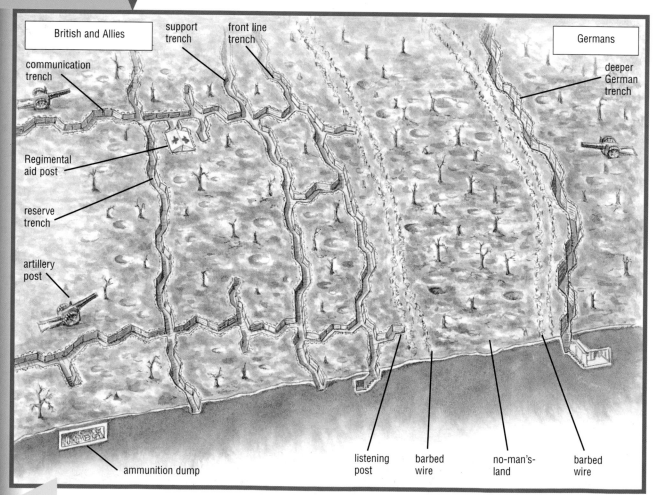

British and Allies

Germans

support trench

front line trench

communication trench

deeper German trench

Regimental aid post

reserve trench

artillery post

ammunition dump

listening post

barbed wire

no-man's-land

barbed wire

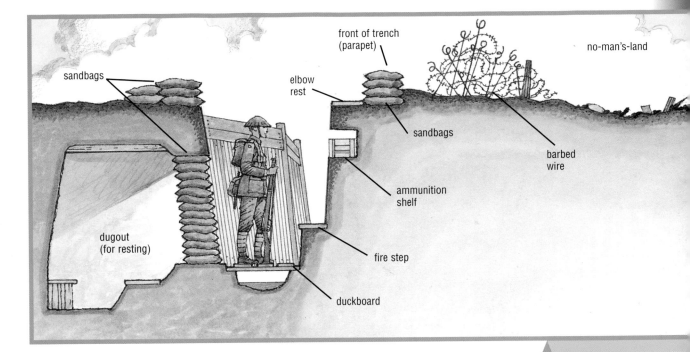

front of trench
(parapet)

no-man's-land

sandbags

elbow
rest

sandbags

barbed
wire

ammunition
shelf

dugout
(for resting)

fire step

duckboard

Trench warfare

A major attack on the enemy lines began with an artillery barrage that usually lasted for days. The idea was to unnerve the enemy and destroy the barbed wire in front of their trenches. Often, however, the shells were duds or fell short and only succeeded in churning up no-man's-land. Sometimes the enemy withdrew from the frontline trench and returned once the gunfire had stopped. After the bombardment, soldiers fixed **bayonets** onto their rifles and went "over the top" of the trench into no-man's-land to attack the enemy trenches. They usually walked straight into a hail of machine-gun fire and were killed by the hundreds. Casualties were very high and gains of land were minimal.

Stretcher-bearers brought back wounded soldiers from no-man's-land. They took them to the Regimental Aid Post, where they were given first aid. Then, the wounded were taken to the **casualty clearing station** behind the lines, where they were operated on if their injuries were serious.

This is a cross-section of a British frontline trench on the Western Front. Sandbags protected the soldiers from enemy fire.

Eyewitnesses

In the daytime you couldn't put your finger above the parapet, let alone your head (for fear of enemy snipers). One young chap jumped on the fire step and looked out across no-man's-land. He was hit in the forehead and was dead before he'd been there three minutes.

Harry Smith, of the British Royal Norfolk Regiment

Brought the wounded down from the front line today. Conditions terrible. The ground is a quagmire. It needs six men to carry each stretcher. The mud was sometimes up to our waists.

From the diary of Sergeant Robert McKay, a British stretcher-bearer in World War I.

Life in the Trenches

Life in the frontline trenches was gruesome. Soldiers usually spent sixteen days on trench duty: eight in the frontline trenches, four in reserve, and four in the rest camp. Even when they were not under attack, the men had to be strong to survive the dreadful conditions.

Conditions in the trenches

In the summer, the trenches were very hot and dusty. But the winters were worse. Heavy rain caused the trenches to flood and men often had to stand knee deep in liquid mud. In frosty weather, the **duckboards,** or paths built of wooden slats that ran along the trenches, would freeze, making it difficult to stand up. Many of the soldiers from the British **Empire** had never seen snow nor felt such cold and were issued woolen underpants. Many men suffered from "trench foot" due to standing in water for long periods. This condition caused the feet to swell and was so painful it made men scream and cry.

Many soldiers suffered from shell shock, a kind of nervous breakdown brought on by fear, stress, and the miserable conditions. Some soldiers were unable to utter a word; others trembled and shook.

It was impossible for soldiers to wash properly, so skin diseases were common. Soldiers' clothes became infested with body lice, causing itchy skin. Men would remove their jackets and run a lit cigarette down the seams in order to burn the eggs of the lice. This gave some relief, but the lice soon returned. Lice also caused trench fever, a kind of flu.

These British soldiers are using a pump to drain a frontline trench in January 1917.

The trenches were also infested with rats, some as large as small cats. They fed off scraps of food and the rotting flesh of dead bodies. The men hated the rats almost as much as the shelling.

The food was not very appetizing. Men lived on tinned corned beef, known in Britain as "bully beef," cookies, bread, and cheese. They were also given tins of Maconochie, a stew which they ate either hot or cold. Sometimes they had bacon and Tommy Tickler's jam, which was jam made of plums and apples. Drinking water was supplied in gas cans and was chlorinated to kill the germs. Not surprisingly, it tasted awful.

This Australian soldier uses a periscope to look out over no-man's-land. His colleagues man the fire step.

Daily routine in the trenches

Life in the **Allied** front line began at dawn with the "daily hate": giving the enemy a volley of rifle and machine-gun fire. The men then had to clean their guns for inspection. After breakfast, there were a variety of jobs to be done. Duckboards had to be repaired or replaced, and sandbags filled. The rest of the day was spent playing cards, reading, writing letters home, and trying to get some much-needed sleep in one of the dugouts. At dusk, food supplies and water were carried up to the front along the communication trenches. At any one time, about a third of the men were on guard duty. This was hard work because it was necessary to be on guard and watch the enemy for two hours at a time.

There was a great deal of activity at night. Some soldiers repaired the barbed wire. Others raided the enemy trenches. Parties of men crawled over **no-man's-land** and threw **grenades** into the enemy trenches. At other times, soldiers crouched in listening posts tried to find out what the enemy was doing.

The relief of trench units also took place at night. The new soldiers, laden down with rolls of barbed wire, shovels, picks, and **corrugated** iron, had to wade through the wet, winding communication trenches. The soldiers coming off trench duty could look forward to a hot bath, a good meal, and some free time in the local town.

The Battle of the Somme, July 1 to November 18, 1916

In 1916, the British and French launched an attack on the German lines along the Somme River in northern France. The British commander, Sir Douglas Haig, aimed to push back the Germans and kill as many enemy soldiers as possible. He believed that a breakthrough could be made in a matter of hours. The attack was also designed to take the pressure off the French who, since February 1916, were desperately defending Verdun, a fortress town in eastern France, from a huge German onslaught.

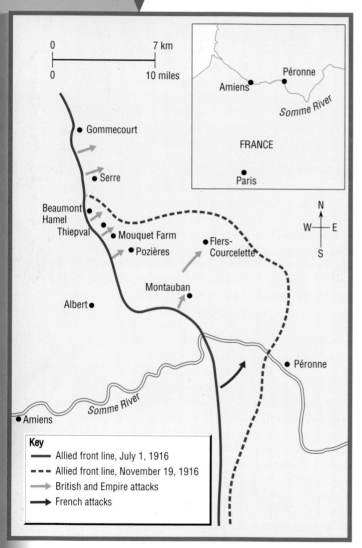

Key
— Allied front line, July 1, 1916
- - - Allied front line, November 19, 1916
→ British and Empire attacks
➤ French attacks

Bombardment

On June 24, 1916, more than 1,500 **Allied** guns began to bombard the German trenches. The barrage went on for seven days. The intention was to "soften up" the Germans and to destroy their trenches and the barbed wire that protected them. In fact, the guns were not powerful enough and many shells landed short of their target, leaving huge craters in **no-man's-land.** It would be difficult for any army to cross.

A day of carnage

On the morning of July 1, 1916, the guns fell silent. It was a fine morning and the birds could be heard singing. At 7:30 A.M., "zero hour," waves of British soldiers were sent over the top. They were told that the artillery bombardment would have destroyed the enemy trenches and they were to walk in straight lines across no-man's-land. It sounded easy.

However, the barbed wire was still in place and the German trenches still intact. The German soldiers had been well sheltered and they emerged from their shelters and manned their machine guns. The advancing British troops were shot immediately. It was utter carnage. In an attack on Serre, the Accrington **pals battalion** lost 584 men out of 720.

CASUALTIES ON THE SOMME	
BRITAIN AND EMPIRE	420,000
FRANCE	200,000
GERMANY	450,000

Near Beaumont Hamel, the Newfoundland Regiment lost 684 men out of 752. At the end of the day, the British casualties stood at 57,470, of which 19,240 were dead. It remains the worst day in British military history.

The campaign continues

In Britain, the newspapers reported on a successful day! Then the full horror of what had happened began to sink in. Haig, however, still believed he could wear down the Germans and he ordered further attacks over the next five months.

On September 15, the British used tanks for the first time in an attack at Flers-Courcelette. They were not very successful. Only 49 were available to Haig and most of them kept breaking down.

This wave of British troops is walking across no-man's-land on July 1, 1916. Another group of soldiers can just be seen waiting in the trenches for their turn to go "over the top."

As winter approached, rainy weather set in and the trenches became very muddy. On November 18, Haig called off the Somme campaign. The Allies had gained only nine mi. (fifteen km) of ground at a massive cost. Haig was criticized for sending so many men to their deaths. But later the Germans said that the battle had taken so much out of their army that it helped toward their eventual defeat in 1918.

A book that stopped a bullet

*We went into the ruined village of Montauban. As we turned a corner there was a German machine-gunner waiting for us. He got me in the foot and I felt two kicks over my heart. I went at him and **bayonetted** him. I sat down to see what the damage was. My foot was bad, but when I looked at my left-hand breast pocket I saw two holes in it. I opened my pocket and found two bullets had gone through my metal shaving mirror and had nosed their way into a book I was carrying. Funnily enough, earlier in the morning my officer had given me the book and said I could read it when I got into the German trenches. So I put it in my pocket, little thinking that I should be able to read it on a hospital ship coming home.*

A British sergeant describes his lucky escape in the *Manchester Guardian*, July 8, 1916.

The Third Battle of Ypres, also known as the Battle of Passchendaele, was fought between July 31 and November 10, 1917.

The plan

In May 1917, Sir Douglas Haig made plans for an all-out **offensive** against the German line near Ypres, in the low-lying area of Flanders, a part of Belgium. He believed that the German army was weakening and now was the time to "break its heart." If the **Allies** could break through the German lines into open country, the way was open to attack the German-occupied ports of Ostend and Zeebrugge, which were key **U-boat** bases. After that, the Allies would advance on Germany itself.

On June 7, 1917, before the battle, the Allies captured the Messines Ridge to the south of Ypres. The attack was then called off. The British prime minister, David Lloyd George, was worried that too many soldiers would be killed. Haig persuaded the prime minister that the attack was needed if Britain was to win the war. He won the argument and in July was allowed to resume the campaign. The delay had given the Germans time to strengthen their trenches with concrete **pillboxes** to prepare for the attack.

At the Third Battle of Ypres, in 1917, the Allies hoped to break through the German lines and capture Ostend and Zeebrugge. Ypres is about 37 mi. (60 km) from Ostend.

The battle begins

On July 16, the Allies began a fifteen-day artillery barrage against the German trenches at Pilckem, to the north of Ypres. More than four million shells were fired. The shells damaged the German trenches and also destroyed the drains and dikes that drained the area of water. At 3:50 A.M. on July 31, General Hubert Gough's men were sent over the top. The weather was terrible. It was pouring rain and the battlefield was like "muddy porridge." The British expected to gain more than two and a half miles (four kilometers) of ground on the first day, but they were pushed back by the Germans, losing 27,000 men in the process.

Pilckem
(July 31)

Passchendaele
(November 10)

Broodseinde
(October 4)

Polygon Wood
(October 3)

Ypres

0   5 km
0   3 miles

English Channel
Zeebrugge
Ostend
BELGIUM
Ypres
FRANCE

→ Intended Allied advance

N
W — E
S

Messines
(June 7)

Key
▨ Higher ground
— Allied front line, July 31
- - - Allied front line, November 10

A sea of mud

August was very wet. With no drainage, the whole area around Ypres became a sea of mud. Still the British continued to attack. By September 25, 3 mi. (5 km) of ground had been won at a cost of 86,000 casualties. The rain continued. Tanks became stuck in the mud, and supplies had to be carried up to the front over slippery planks of wood. Stretcher-bearers were hampered by the thick mud in **no-man's-land.** Hundreds of wounded soldiers drowned before help could get to them. In early October, the weather improved and British and **ANZAC (Australian and New Zealand Army Corps)** troops gained territory at Polygon Wood and Broodseinde.

These stretcher-bearers, knee deep in mud, struggle to rescue a wounded man from no-man's-land during the Third Battle of Ypres, 1917.

Passchendaele falls

In late October, Canadian troops launched an attack on the village of Passchendaele, which was situated on a ridge of higher ground. If this ridge was captured, the Allies would have a dry spot to spend the winter. At 6:00 A.M. on November 6, the Canadians went "over the top." The fighting was fierce, but they managed to capture the now ruined village. On November 10, the Allied forces called off the campaign.

Altogether, five miles (eight kilometers) of ground had been gained in three and a half months of fighting. Haig's aim of breaking through the German lines and into open country had not been achieved. The Allies and the Germans had both lost about 300,000 men. Germany lost some of its best soldiers and morale was now very low in its army.

Technology and New Weapons

World War I was fought between **industrialized** countries that had scientists and engineers capable of making weapons of mass destruction. During the war, two new weapons were produced which were meant to break the deadlock of trench warfare. They had mixed success.

Tanks

In 1912, an Australian, L.E. Moles, suggested building an armor-plated, bullet-proof vehicle with guns that could be used to bulldoze through enemy lines. He was ignored! When World War I broke out, a British soldier, Colonel Ernest Swinton, persuaded Winston Churchill, then the First Lord of the Admiralty, to look at the idea again. Swinton argued that an armored vehicle with caterpillar tracks would be able to travel over rough ground and smash through barbed wire and trenches. It could also knock out the enemy's machine guns, allowing the **infantry** to move in.

This early British tank moves at Thiepval during the Battle of the Somme on September 25, 1916.

In 1915, a model tank called *Little Willie* was built, and from this the first really useful *Mark I* tank was developed. In February 1916, the *Mark I* was demonstrated to **Lord Kitchener,** the minister for war, in Hatfield Park, north of London. He was not impressed and said it would never win the war. However, Sir Douglas Haig thought it was worth trying and, in September 1916, 49 tanks were used in the Battle of the Somme. Unfortunately, they were very slow, kept breaking down, and clearly had problems. Haig still thought they had potential and asked the British government to supply the army with 1,000 more tanks.

In 1917, the faster *Whippet* tank was built and successfully used in the Battle of Cambrai, the first time that tanks were used in force. In 1918, the British and Americans jointly produced the *Mark VIII*, or *Liberty*, tank. It weighed 41 tons (37 tonnes), carried a crew of 8, and could fire 208 shells and 13,000 bullets. The main difference between it and earlier tanks was that the engine was separated from the crew's compartment. Although not yet perfect, the tank had shown itself to be a weapon for the future.

Poisonous gases

Chlorine gas was first used by the Germans in April 1915. Containers of gas were opened and it was allowed to drift toward the enemy. The problem for the attacking side was that if the wind changed direction, the gas could be blown back toward them. Gas was meant to disrupt the enemy before an attack was made, and it succeeded. The first gas attacks caused panic among enemy troops. They had never experienced anything like it before. Chlorine gas filled the lungs with fluid, and this often resulted in death from suffocation.

The British soon developed their own chlorine gas, which they used against the Germans in the Battle of Loos in September 1915. By 1917, the Germans were using mustard gas. This was much more deadly, causing sickness, internal bleeding, blindness, and burning of the skin. By now, gas was fired in shells from long-range guns, so it did not matter from which direction the wind was blowing.

In this painting, American artist John Singer Sargent captured the effects of mustard gas on World War I troops.

Initially, soldiers protected themselves from gas by wearing goggles and putting handkerchiefs soaked in urine over their mouths. Later, face masks with air tubes and filters were introduced and, although they gave better protection, they made it difficult for the soldiers to breathe and move. During the war, more than 91,000 soldiers were killed by gas and a further 1,200,000 were injured by it.

GAS PRODUCTION IN WORLD WAR I	
GERMANY	76,000 TONS (69,000 TONNES)
FRANCE	42,000 TONS (38,000 TONNES)
BRITAIN	28,000 TONS (25,000 TONNES)

Not a joy ride!

Tanks were terribly noisy, oily, hot, airless and bumpy! As they had no springs and weighed 33 tons (30 tonnes), any slight bump was magnified, throwing the crew about. If the tank was hit in action, pieces of hot steel flew around. Bullets hitting the armored plates caused the steel to melt and splash. It was dangerous to the eyes.

A British tank commander describing what it was like inside a World War I tank.

The Battle of Cambrai, November 20, 1917

In August 1917, Colonel John Fuller of the British Tank Corps suggested a massed tank attack on the German lines to the southwest of Cambrai in northern France. The land here was made up of gentle chalk hills and was well drained and dry. It was ideal terrain for tanks. After some discussion, Sir Douglas Haig, commander-in-chief of the British army, agreed, and planning for the Battle of Cambrai began in earnest.

The plan

The attack on the German lines would be made up of four phases.

1. An advance line of tanks would move into **no-man's-land** and crush the barbed wire protecting the German trenches.
2. The main group of tanks would follow and cross the German trenches by dropping their **fascines** into them.
3. The **infantry** would then move in and clear the German trenches of any enemy soldiers.
4. The **cavalry** would burst through the gaps made in the trenches and surround the town of Cambrai.

Preparations

The date for the attack was to be November 20, 1917. For two weeks before the attack, the British soldiers underwent detailed training. The Tank Corps was anxious to succeed. So far, the performance of the tank in battle had been disappointing and many generals did not think it was much help. Tanks were transported to the battlefield at night by railway and hidden from the view of the Germans. It was decided not to have the usual preliminary artillery barrage, as this would warn the Germans that an attack was imminent.

A painting by W.L. Wyllie shows British tanks rolling into action at Cambrai.

The battle

At 6:20 A.M., more than 1,000 British guns started to bombard the German trenches, and immediately the first of 378 British tanks rumbled into no-man's-land. They were supported by 289 aircraft that attacked enemy gun batteries. The tanks moved forward, crushing barbed wire and crossing over the German trenches. The Germans had been taken by surprise and were powerless to stop the advance. At the end of the day, four miles (six kilometers) of territory had been gained over a six-mile (ten-kilometer) front. The supporting infantry had taken 6,000 prisoners. When England heard the news, church bells were rung in celebration.

It was not a complete success, as 179 tanks had been lost either to enemy gunfire or because of mechanical breakdown. Some got stuck trying to cross the trenches. By November 23, only 92 tanks were working and there were none in reserve to keep up the pressure. When the cavalry moved in, they were driven back by German gunfire. There was also not enough infantry in reserve.

The Germans moved reinforcements into the area, and on November 30 launched a fierce counterattack, using artillery, aircraft, and gas. They managed to win back nearly all of the ground they had lost. At the end of the fighting, both sides had lost about 45,000 men. Although it was not a decisive victory, the tanks had proven their worth and shown they were a weapon of the future. For the tank, the Battle of Cambrai was a turning point.

Dry ground was ideally suited for these British tanks, as they attack during the Battle of Cambrai.

Tanks go into battle

My tank was in the second wave of attack. At 6:30 A.M., I gave the "right away" and our engine purred with perfect tuning. As the mist cleared I found it possible to recognize all the features shown on the air photos and maps, and the going was easy over the rolling grassy slopes. Our infantry waved us on. The enemy fire withered and it became clear that the fantastic sight of all our monsters approaching had demoralized the Germans. Our infantry had little to do but to receive the prisoners and clear the dugouts in the trenches.

Lieutenant Gordon Hassell of the Tank Corps describes the first day of the Battle of Cambrai.

Women on the Western Front

This 1915 recruitment poster is for the Voluntary Aid Detachment.

Women were not allowed to fight, but this did not prevent them from going to the **Western Front** to provide vital support for soldiers. Women from all the **Allied** countries were eager to show their patriotism and to prove they were the equals of men. Besides the Western Front, women also served on the **Eastern Front,** in Gallipoli and the Middle East.

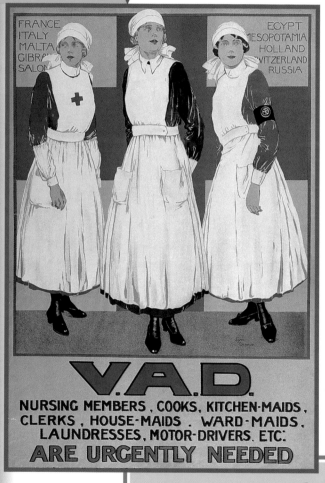

FRANCE ITALY MALTA GIBRA SALON

EGYPT MESOPOTAMIA HOLLAND SWITZERLAND RUSSIA

V.A.D.

NURSING MEMBERS , COOKS, KITCHEN-MAIDS , CLERKS , HOUSE-MAIDS . WARD-MAIDS , LAUNDRESSES, MOTOR-DRIVERS. ETC:

ARE URGENTLY NEEDED

Women's organizations

The First Aid Nursing Yeomanry (FANYs) enlisted women to support the troops in Belgium and France. They helped out as nurses in field hospitals, drove ambulances, and set up troop **canteens.** The Voluntary Aid Detachment (VADs) sent more than 8,000 women to northern France to work as nurses, mechanics, ambulance drivers, clerical workers, cleaners, and cooks. To begin with, VADs were looked down upon by the soldiers and nicknamed "Very Active Dusters"! But very soon, as with all women at the front, they won respect and admiration for the work they did.

More than 16,000 U.S. women flocked to Europe to help the Allied war effort. They worked as nurses, secretaries, welfare workers, and canteen workers. In 1918, over 200 highly trained U.S. women served with

Sister Pearl Corkhill

Pearl Corkhill was an Australian nurse working close to the front line in a **casualty clearing station.** In July 1918, German aircraft twice bombed the clearing station. Pearl was awarded the Military Medal for her bravery. She wrote to her mother to tell her the news:

Today word came that I had been awarded the Military Medal. Well the Commanding Officer sent over a bottle of champagne and they all drank my health and now the medical officers are giving me a dinner in honor of the event. I can't see what I've done to deserve it but the part I don't like is having to face old George and Mary [the king and queen] to get the medal. It will cost me a new mess dress, but I suppose I should not grumble at that—I'm still wearing the one I left Australia in.

the U.S. Signal Corps. Nicknamed "hello girls," they worked as telephone operators in France. The Australian Army Nursing Service sent over 2,000 nurses to Europe to serve in military hospitals.

Hardship and danger

Women support workers at the front had to put up with the same conditions

as the soldiers. They lived in huts and tents with few comforts. Women were also in danger of being gassed or shelled. In 1917, a military hospital run by U.S. nurses was bombed, causing the deaths of several patients and injuring nurses. Elsie Grey, a New Zealand nurse, described in her diary how a shell hit the tents they were living in: "The shell burst and a piece of shrapnel shot through the tent piercing an artery of a British nurse. Ten minutes later she was dead." One VAD grew so distressed at the number of wounded soldiers she saw that she jumped off a cliff and killed herself. Disease and illness were also a problem. Many women suffered from exhaustion, lice, shell shock, and influenza.

A bomb attack on their living quarters in Étaples, France, killed two Canadian nurses. Those who survived are shown cleaning up the damage.

The Madonnas of Pervyse

In 1914, two British women, Mairi Chisholm and Elsie Knocker, went to Belgium to work as ambulance drivers. Together they set up a first aid station very close to the front line at Pervyse. They went into **no-man's-land,** often under fire, to bring back wounded soldiers. They treated the soldiers at their first aid post before sending them on to a military hospital. Soldiers looked after by Mairi and Elsie knew they were in good hands and nicknamed them "the two Madonnas of Pervyse." In March 1918, both women were gassed during a German attack. Only then did they return to Britain after four years of heroic work.

The Gallipoli Campaign, 1915

In October 1914, Turkey entered the war on the side of Germany. By early 1915, there was a stalemate on the **Western Front,** so the British government decided to attack Turkey. If Turkey was forced out of the war, the **Allies** could attack Austria-Hungary from the south and send supplies through the Black Sea to Russia.

The plan was to send a fleet of ships to force its way through the Straits of Dardanelles, a narrow stretch of water that leads into the Black Sea. Once through the Straits, the ships would advance on Constantinople and force Turkey to surrender. The Straits were guarded on either side by Turkish forts and guns. The British believed that the Turks would not fight very hard and that their guns were out of date. In February and March 1915, British and French ships bombarded the Turkish forts and tried to sail through the Straits. They were forced back by gunfire and **minefields.** Three ships were sunk by mines, and three were badly damaged, with a loss of 700 men.

The Gallipoli Campaign in Turkey lasted for eight months in 1915. Despite the bravery of the Allied troops, the campaign ended in failure.

April 25, 1915—a day to forget

A change of plan was called for. It was decided to land troops on the Gallipoli peninsula and capture the Turkish forts. Then the ships would be able to sail through the Straits unopposed. On April 25, 1915, a force of British, French, Indian, and **ANZAC** soldiers, commanded by General Sir Ian Hamilton, landed on the narrow beaches of Gallipoli.

Unfortunately, the British commanders had not done enough planning. The troops were short of guns and there was no specialist landing craft. Instead, the troops were put ashore in row boats. There were no engineers and equipment to build a pier so that supplies could be landed quickly. The officers in charge did not account for the steep cliffs that rose up from some of the beaches. The Turks had positioned machine gun units on top of the cliffs. As the Allied troops clambered up the cliffs, they came under heavy fire and suffered terrible casualties.

AUSTRIA-HUNGARY

ITALY

TURKEY

Suvla Bay

Sairi Bair Hills

▲ Chunuk Bair

ANZAC Cove

Lone Pine Ridge

Aegean Sea

Gallipoli Peninsula

Straits of Dardanelles

Cape Helles

Furthest point reached by Allied ships

Key
- Highland
- Turkish minefields
- ◆ Turkish forts
- • Smaller Turkish guns
- → Naval advance, Feb/March
- → British landings, April 25
- → ANZAC landings, April 25
- → British landings, August 6
- → ANZAC attacks, August 6
- Ground gained by Allies

0   4 km
0   3 miles

N
W—E
S

The fiasco continues

The Allies advanced just three miles (five kilometers) before digging themselves into trenches. It was stalemate again, just like the Western Front. Dead bodies lay everywhere. The smell of rotting flesh was so strong that a truce was called so that the dead could be buried. The hot summer sun beat down on the Allied soldiers. Water was in short supply, and flies and lice were everywhere. Soon, 200 men a day were falling sick with dysentery, fever, and typhoid.

On August 6, Allied reinforcements landed at Suvla Bay. They fought bravely but, once again, the determined Turks beat them back and stopped them from advancing inland. The Allies were again forced to dig trenches to defend themselves. By November, winter had set in and soldiers began to die of frostbite. It was clear that the invasion of Gallipoli had failed. In December, the disastrous campaign was called off. By January 9, 1916, the surviving 135,000 Allied troops had been evacuated in a brilliant operation. This was the only success of a disastrous campaign. The Allies had lost 265,000 men, including 36,000 ANZAC troops.

ANZAC troops land at the cove named after them on April 25, 1915. The steep cliffs overlooking the narrow beach are clearly visible.

Terrible injuries

Men had lost arms and legs, brains oozed out of skulls, and lungs protruded from riven chests; many had lost their faces. One poor chap had lost his nose and we also had to take off an arm, a hand, and extract two bullets like shark's teeth from his thigh. I saw him the next morning being carried to the mortuary.

A medical orderly describes the injuries received by the Allied forces on April 25, 1915.

The ANZACS

ANZAC was short for the Australian and New Zealand Army Corps. The Australian troops were nicknamed "diggers" and were famous for their courage and cheerfulness during the heat of battle. In Australia and New Zealand, the heroism and sacrifices of the troops at Gallipoli are remembered each year on April 25—ANZAC Day.

The Landings at Suvla Bay, 1915

In the summer of 1915, the fighting in Gallipoli was deadlocked. Both sides had dug trenches and were defending their positions. In August, Sir Ian Hamilton decided to attack the Turks again in an effort to win control of the Gallipoli peninsula. It was to be a two-pronged attack. Australian and New Zealand troops were to leave their base at **ANZAC** Cove and attack the Turkish guns in the Sairi Bair hills. Five miles (eight kilometers) farther north fresh British troops were to be landed on the poorly defended beaches of Suvla Bay.

The Australians at Lone Pine Ridge

On the afternoon of August 6, 1915, the Australians, under **General Sir William Birdwood,** attacked the Turkish trenches at Lone Pine Ridge. They were inexperienced soldiers but they fought with great courage. The fighting was hand to hand, with rifles and **bayonets.** Dead bodies soon filled the trenches. One soldier said, "It was like one big grave, only some of us were still alive in it." By the evening, the Australians had captured the ridge. They held it for three days before the Turks fought back and regained some of the ground. The Australians lost 2,273 men during the action. New Zealand forces won some territory at nearby Chunuk Bair before they, too, were pushed back by the Turks.

ANZAC troops are charging Turkish machine gun positions.

Suvla Bay

Also on August 6, British troops landed at Suvla Bay. They met little resistance from the Turks. Once ashore, the troops were not sure what to do! Sir Ian Hamilton was at his headquarters aboard a ship anchored off the coast. If he had told the troops to attack the Turks immediately, they could have linked up with the Australians and New Zealanders and gained control of the peninsula. But there was a complete breakdown in communications. Some of the British troops went for a swim while they waited for orders. By the time Hamilton did order an attack, it was too late. The Turks had brought in reinforcements, and they were able to hold off the British. Although the British and ANZACs did link up, they were unable to take any more territory.

In October 1915, Hamilton was fired and replaced as commander by *Sir Charles Monro*. Two months later, the Gallipoli campaign was abandoned.

Named after Queen Victoria, the Victoria Cross was first awarded during the Crimean War in 1857.

THE VICTORIA CROSS

THE VICTORIA CROSS IS BRITAIN'S HIGHEST AWARD FOR GALLANTRY IN WAR. DURING THE GALLIPOLI CAMPAIGN, TEN ANZAC SOLDIERS WERE AWARDED THE VICTORIA CROSS.

DATE	NAME	COUNTRY	PLACE
MAY 20, 1915	ALBERT JACKA	AUSTRALIA	COURTNEY'S POST
AUGUST 7, 1915	CYRIL BASSETT	NEW ZEALAND	CHUNUK BAIR
AUGUST 7, 1915	LEONARD KEYSOR	AUSTRALIA	LONE PINE
AUGUST 8, 1915	WILLIAM SYMONS	AUSTRALIA	LONE PINE
AUGUST 9, 1915	ALEXANDER BURTON	AUSTRALIA	LONE PINE
AUGUST 9, 1915	WILLIAM DUNSTAN	AUSTRALIA	LONE PINE
AUGUST 9, 1915	JOHN HAMILTON	AUSTRALIA	LONE PINE
AUGUST 9, 1915	ALFRED SHOUT	AUSTRALIA	LONE PINE
AUGUST 9, 1915	FRED TUBB	AUSTRALIA	LONE PINE
AUGUST 30, 1915	HUGO THROSSELL	AUSTRALIA	HILL 60

Keith Murdoch

People in Britain, Australia, and New Zealand did not know about the bad planning and incompetence of the generals in Gallipoli. The truth was kept from them. The army authorities censored all newspaper articles sent from Gallipoli.

Keith Murdoch, an Australian journalist, went to Gallipoli in the summer of 1915. He was shocked that fighting was still going on. Murdoch believed that the land was so steep that it was obvious that the Allies would not be able to win much territory. Hamilton, he said, should have called off the fighting after the landings of April 25, 1915.

Murdoch went to England in September 1915. From here he wrote a long letter to Andrew Fisher, the Australian prime minister. He told the true story of Gallipoli: the pointless fighting, the lack of planning, and the disease among the troops. Fisher told the British government, who, in turn, allowed the information to be published in newspapers. This led many people to call for the troops to be withdrawn from Gallipoli.

The Eastern Front, 1914–1917

The Russians, with an army of five million men, thought they would quickly steamroll the Germans and Austrians to defeat on the **Eastern Front.** But things did not quite turn out as they expected.

The Battle of Tannenberg, August 26–30, 1914

In August 1914, two large Russian armies under **General Pavel Rennenkampf** and **General Alexander Samsonov** invaded East Prussia, a part of Germany. The two generals did not like each other, and were not on speaking terms. Hardly a recipe for success! The plan was for the two armies to split to go around the Masurian Lakes. Once past the lakes, they would attack the Germans from two sides and move on to Berlin. The Germans, however, picked up the plan on their radios and knew what was happening.

The Eastern Front involved fighting between Russia and Germany and Austria-Hungary from 1914 to 1917.

At Tannenberg, Samsonov's army was surrounded by the Germans. Thousands of Russians were driven into swamplands. As they struggled in the water, the Germans machine-gunned them to death. Samsonov was so upset, he shot himself. About 30,000 Russians were killed and a further 100,000 taken prisoner. Between September 7 and 14, Rennenkampf was beaten in the Battle of the Masurian Lakes, losing 100,000 men. The Russians were forced to retreat.

The Russians had been beaten because they were poorly organized and were short of weapons and ammunition. The Germans were much better organized and equipped. But the Russian **offensive** had caused the Germans to move thousands of troops from the **Western Front,** helping the British and French win the Battle of the Marne in September 1914.

Key

✗	Major battles
→	Russian attacks in 1914
→	Russian attacks led by Brusilov, 1916
→	German attacks, 1914–15
—	Front line, December 1917
- - -	Front line, December 1914

Baltic Sea
EAST PRUSSIA
Masurian Lakes, 1914
Tannenberg, 1914
Berlin
GERMANY
Brest Litovsk
POLAND
RUSSIA
Galicia
Vienna
AUSTRIA-HUNGARY
ROMANIA
Black Sea

0 — 500 km
0 — 300 miles

N
W — E
S

Slaughter!

This is not war, it is slaughter. Hundreds of thousands of our men are without weapons and have to wait until they can pick up rifles dropped by fallen comrades.

A Russian politician gives his view on the Battle of Tannenberg.

Meanwhile, another Russian army won a decisive victory over the Austrians in Galicia. In the Battle of Lemberg, August 26 to September 10, 1914, the Austrians were forced to retreat over 149 mi. (240 km) and suffered 250,000 casualties.

Brusilov strikes back

In the summer of 1915, the Germans and Austrians forced the Russians to retreat farther. Thousands of peasants were turned out of their homes and had to flee with the army. The peasants were dressed in summer clothes and when winter came, many froze to death. **Czar Nicholas II,** fed up with the poor performance of his army generals, made himself commander-in-chief of the Russian army. In February 1916, he ordered a counterattack against the Germans. It failed, and the Russian losses were high. Food was scarce inside Russia and prices skyrocketed. People were growing tired of both the czar and the war.

In June 1916, General Alexei Brusilov attacked the Austrians near the Romanian border. For a change, his army had plenty of weapons and ammunition. Brusilov gained about 62 mi. (100 km) of territory before his troops became exhausted and the advance ground to a halt.

The Russian Revolution: Russia pulls out of the war

The Germans sent reinforcements to the Eastern Front and once again pushed the Russian army back. By now, the Russians were tired and lacking in spirit. They began to desert the army by the thousands. The czar's popularity was at an all-time low. The people blamed him for the plight of the country, and there were strikes and riots in the major cities. In March 1917, the czar was forced to resign from the throne. In November 1917, the **Bolsheviks** seized power, executed the czar, and turned Russia into a communist country. The new Bolshevik government, led by Lenin, immediately pulled Russia out of the war and, on March 3, 1918, signed the **Treaty of Brest Litovsk** with Germany. For Russia itself, the war had been a disaster, but without the Russian army occupying the Germans in the east, the Allies could have lost the war on the Western Front.

This photograph shows Czar Nicholas II with Russian troops on the Eastern Front. By early 1917, the war had ruined the Russian economy, making the czar very unpopular.

Mutiny!

We throw our rifles away, because things are dreadful in our army, and so are our officers.

A Russian soldier, 1916

Side-show Fronts

The side-show fronts were smaller battlegrounds, away from the **Western** and **Eastern Fronts,** in other parts of Europe and around the world.

War in the colonies

Germany lost nearly all its **colonies** to **Allied** forces during the war. In the Pacific, New Zealanders took German Samoa in August 1914, and the Australians captured German New Guinea two weeks later. Japanese troops overran the German trading station at Kiaochow in China, as well as the Marshall, Caroline, and Marianas Islands.

In Africa, the Allies captured Togoland, German Southwest Africa, and the Cameroons. Only German East Africa—now Tanzania—remained in German hands. Here, General Lettow-Vorbeck managed to beat off the Allied attacks.

The Italian front, 1915–1918, involved fighting in mountainous areas, with troops on both sides showing great courage.

The Italian front

The Italians joined the Allies in May 1915, hoping to gain land from the Austrians. The two sides fought each other along a front on Italy's northeastern border with Austria-Hungary. The area is mountainous, and fighting was made dangerous by ice, snow blizzards, and fog. In November 1917, German troops were sent to help the Austrians. Together they smashed the Italians at the Battle of Caporetto, pushing them back 62 mi. (100 km).

The map shows:
AUSTRIA-HUNGARY
The Alps
ITALY
Caporetto, 1917
Vittorio Veneto, 1918
Piave River
Isonzo River
Garda Lake
N
W — E
S
Venice
Gulf of Venice

Key
Land occupied by Italy, 1915–17
Front line, December 1917

0   75 km
0   50 miles

The Italians lost at least 250,000 men and a further 400,000 soldiers deserted. The Italian army was near total collapse. Britain and France sent troops to help. It was not until late 1918 that the Italians were strong enough to mount another attack, when they beat the Austrians at the Battle of Vittorio Veneto.

War in the Middle East

Germany's ally, Turkey, controlled a large amount of land in the Middle East. Britain was worried that the Turks would cut off its oil supplies and block the Suez Canal. More than a million British, Australian, New

Zealand, and Indian troops were sent to the area to fight the Turks. In December 1915, the Turks trapped an Allied force inside the town of Kut in Mesopotamia—now Iraq. The town was put under siege and food supplies began to run out. In April 1916, the Allied troops were forced to surrender. More than 12,000 men were captured. Half of them died in prison camps. After this, the Allies fought back and took the city of Baghdad in 1917.

Meanwhile, a force led by General Edmund Allenby, formerly guarding the Suez Canal, began an advance on Palestine (modern-day Israel). They pushed the Turks back and captured Jerusalem on December 9, 1917. In September 1918, the Turks were beaten by Allenby at Megiddo. By now, the Turks had had enough and pulled out of the war on October 31.

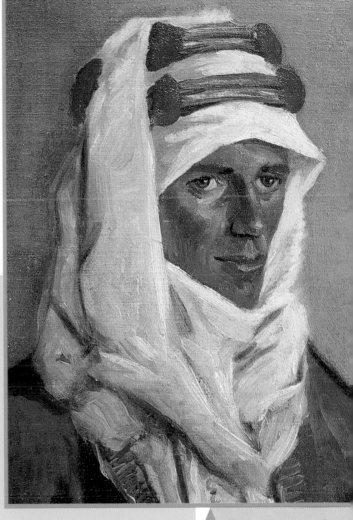

Lawrence of Arabia

Thomas Edward Lawrence, nicknamed "Ned" by his family, was born in Wales in 1888. He studied history at Oxford University, and from 1910 to 1914 worked as an archaeologist in Mesopotamia. It was here that he learned to speak Arabic and learned the Arab way of life. In 1914, he joined the British army and was sent to serve in Egypt. When the Arabs revolted against their Turkish rulers in 1916, Lawrence was sent to advise them. He quickly won the respect and admiration of the Arab leaders, dressing in Arab clothes and living as one of them. Lawrence led the Arabs in a number of **guerrilla** attacks on the Damascus-Medina railway, the main supply line of the Turkish army. He also captured the port of Akaba from the Turks in 1917, which helped pave the way for Allenby's forces to invade Palestine. The Turks put up a reward of £20,000 for his capture, a huge amount at the time. They actually caught him on one occasion but did not realize who he was. Lawrence was killed in a motorcycle accident in Dorset, England, in 1935.

This painting of Thomas Edward Lawrence shows how he dressed in Arab clothes. After the war, Lawrence worked for the British as an adviser on Arab affairs.

War at Sea: Battle of Jutland, May 31, 1916

Before the war, both Britain and Germany had built up large navies, which included the new **Dreadnought**-class battleships. But in 1914, the Germans kept their fleet in port, not wanting to risk their expensive ships in a big naval battle.

In August 1914, the Germans had several squadrons of ships in overseas waters. This led to a number of small fights with **Allied** ships. On November 1, a German squadron under Admiral von Spee destroyed two British ships at Coronel off the coast of Chile. Revenge for the British came on December 8, when Admiral Sturdee sank four out of five of von Spee's warships off the Falkland Islands, near Argentina. In the meantime, the Australian cruiser *Sydney* sank the German cruiser *Emden*, which had been attacking Allied shipping in the Indian Ocean. These victories cleared the seas of German warships, and troops from all over the British Empire could sail to Europe without being attacked.

Blockade

The Battle of Jutland in 1916 was the only major naval battle to take place in World War I.

The British navy now had control of the sea and it blockaded German ports to stop food supplies from reaching Germany. The German High Seas fleet stayed in port. Occasionally, German **battle-cruisers** sailed into the North Sea to bombard towns on the east coast of England, causing civilian casualties. In January 1915, a small naval battle took place on the Dogger Bank, which resulted in the sinking of the *Blucher*, a German battle-cruiser. A major battle, however, was soon to follow.

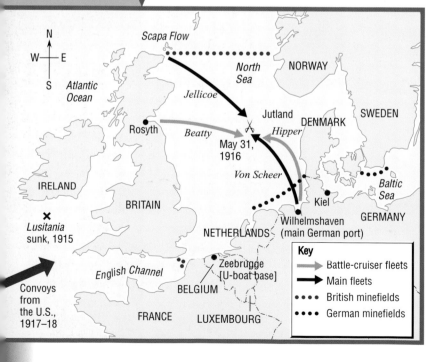

The Battle of Jutland, May 31, 1916

In early 1916, Admiral von Scheer took over command of the German High Seas fleet. He wanted to see action! On May 31, he ordered a group of battle-cruisers, commanded by Admiral Hipper, to sail into the North Sea. The German plan was to tempt the British Grand Fleet out into open sea and attack it by surprise. The British knew what was happening because they had a copy of the German codebook. A squadron of British battle-cruisers, led by Admiral Beatty, was sent to meet the German ships. The two main fleets of battleships followed behind the battle-cruisers. At 4:00 P.M. the two sets of battle-cruisers met off the coast of Jutland near Denmark. Within 30 minutes, the British ship *Indefatigable* exploded and sank. More than 1,000 sailors went down with it, dying from explosions, drowning, or burning to death. Shortly afterward, the *Queen Mary* also exploded and sank within 90 seconds, with a loss of 1,268 men. A mere eight men were rescued from the water. A shocked Admiral Beatty was heard to say, "There seems to be something wrong with our bloody ships today!"

BATTLE FACTS: BATTLE OF JUTLAND		
	BRITAIN	GERMANY
NUMBER OF SHIPS	151	103
SHIPS LOST	14	11
MEN KILLED	6,100	2,550

At 6:00 P.M., the two main fleets joined the battle. More than 250 ships were involved in the exchange of gunfire. Huge battleships fired shells that weighed a ton each. Von Scheer realized he was outnumbered and turned for home. The weather was misty, so Admiral Sir John Jellicoe did not chase him. He feared the Germans were luring them toward a pack of **U-boats** and a **minefield.** The battle was over.

Who won?

Both sides claimed victory. The Germans said they had won because they had sunk more ships and lost fewer men. The British said they were the winners because they still had control of the North Sea and the blockade of Germany was still intact. The British were right, for the German High Seas fleet stayed in port for the rest of the war.

This is a painting of John Travers Cornwell during the Battle of Jutland.

The Boy Sailor: John Travers Cornwell

Cornwell was sixteen years old and a gunner onboard the light cruiser, HMS *Chester*, which was hit seventeen times by German shells during the Battle of Jutland. He was badly wounded along with many around him. Despite this, he continued to try to fire shells at the German ships. He died from his wounds in England on June 2, 1916. He was later awarded the Victoria Cross, which was presented to his mother by King George V.

War under the Sea: The U-boat Threat

In 1914, German submarines, known as **U-boats,** sank three British warships in the English Channel. When allowed to roam, U-boats were deadly. They surprised ships by firing torpedoes, or they used their guns while on the surface. The British did not want to risk their warships against the U-boats and always used a screen of **destroyers** to protect them when at sea. Despite this, U-boats were a powerful weapon for Germany.

The U-boat campaign begins

Most of Britain's supplies came across the sea either from the United States or from countries in the **empire.** Germany knew that if enough supply ships going to Britain could be sunk, Britain would be forced to surrender. Early in the war, the U-boats only attacked ships from countries at war with Germany. Then, on February 4, 1915, the Germans started to attack ships from all countries, whether they were in the war or not. This was called unrestricted submarine warfare.

On May 7, the British liner *Lusitania* was sunk by a U-boat off the coast of Ireland. The Germans believed—rightly—that it was carrying munitions and passengers to Britain. Among the 1,198 people who died were 128 Americans. The United States was **neutral** at this time and the country was outraged. After this, there were fewer U-boat attacks because the Germans were fearful that the powerful United States might declare war.

A U-boat attacks an Allied ship

After many alterations of course and speed the destroyer passes within 60 yds. (60 m) of us. "Slow ahead!" A look at the torpedo sight on the periscope. Four more degrees until we can fire. "It's a troopship! Lots of soldiers on board!" whispers the captain. "Up periscope!" "No. 1 tube ready!" The periscope rises and the captain looks into it, with his hat pushed back on his head. "Fire! Dive to 100 ft. [30m]! Down periscope!" The torpedo speeds on its way. Twenty seconds later: a hit! The ship is sinking.

Martin Niemoller, a U-boat crew member

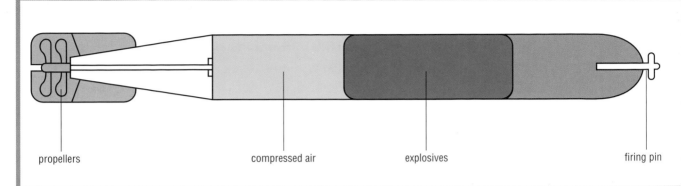

propellers   compressed air   explosives   firing pin

Crisis

By 1917, the Germans were anxious to force a victory. They themselves were suffering from food shortages because the British navy had blockaded German ports. On February 1, they started unrestricted submarine warfare again, a decision that contributed to the United States declaring war on April 6, 1917. By now there were 200 U-boats at sea causing havoc with **Allied** and neutral ships. In April 1917, almost 992,000 tons (900,000 tonnes) of Allied ships were sunk. Soon, Britain had just six weeks of food supplies left. Admiral Jellicoe said, "It is impossible to go on with the war if losses like this continue."

Fighting the U-boats

One way to fight the U-boat was the use of Q-ships. These were merchant ships with hidden guns on their decks. If a U-boat surfaced, it was taken by surprise when the Q-ship's guns were uncovered. The Germans soon grew wise to this, and the Q-ships lost their effectiveness.

The British laid a barrage of 500 mines across the Straits of Dover. This stopped the U-boats from passing through the English Channel and into the Atlantic. Instead, they had to go the long way around the north of Scotland. **Depth charges** were also fired at U-boats. The best way of countering the U-boats was the convoy system, introduced by David Lloyd George, the British prime minister, in April 1917. Merchant vessels were grouped together and escorted across the sea by destroyers. The U.S. Navy aided in this operation by providing destroyers to ensure the merchant ships reached safety. It proved to be very effective. The number of U-boats destroyed increased and the loss of Allied ships was reduced. This saved Britain from being starved into surrender. But it was a close call.

A World War I torpedo was a deadly weapon. It had a range of 32,808 ft. (10,000 m) and was powered by a compressed air engine. It also had a mechanism to control its direction.

NUMBER OF U-BOATS DESTROYED	
1914–16	46
1917	63
1918	69

NUMBER OF ALLIED SHIPS SUNK BY U-BOATS	
1914	3
1915	396
1916	964
1917	2,439
1918	1,035

War in the Air

In 1914, aircraft design was still in its infancy. Airplanes were made of wood and canvas and were very flimsy. They were powered by unreliable engines that often shut off in the air. Pilots had to be brave. They took their lives into their hands on every flight! By 1918, aircraft design had made great strides. Although airplanes did not have any great effect on the outcome of the war, it was clear that they would change how armies fought wars in the future.

Reconnaissance and observation

No one really knew what part airplanes would play in the war. One British general said they were "useless and an expensive fad!" They were used mainly for reconnaissance, or observation, flights over enemy lines. An observer sitting behind the pilot made sketches and took photographs of trench systems and troop movements. At sea, aircraft were used to spot enemy ships and U-boats.

Fighters and air aces

Soon, pilots began taking pistols and rifles in the air, hoping to take a quick shot at an enemy plane. Then, in 1915, Anthony Fokker, a Dutch aircraft designer working for the Germans, invented a synchronized gear that enabled a machine gun to fire bullets through the moving propeller blades. This led to the production of fighter planes and to high-speed, one-to-one aerial battles called "dogfights." Pilots would chase an enemy plane and fire a hail of bullets.

Allied pilots with more than five kills were known as "aces." German pilots did not receive "ace" status until they had ten kills. "Aces" were looked upon as heroes whose adventures were widely reported in newspapers. As the war went on, fighter aircraft became faster, more reliable, and

This painting depicts a dogfight over the town of Arras in northern France.

LEADING FIGHTER ACES		
NAME	COUNTRY	NUMBER OF "KILLS"
MANFRED VON RICHTHOFEN ("THE RED BARON")	GERMANY	80
RENÉ FONCK	FRANCE	75
MICK MANNOCK	U.K.	73
WILLIAM BISHOP	CANADA	72
ROBERT A. LITTLE	AUSTRALIA	47
EDWARD RICKENBACKER	UNITED STATES	26

capable of staying in the air for more than two hours. In 1918, the main British fighter, the *Sopwith Camel*, could climb to 18,944 ft. (5,774 m) and had a speed of 115 mph (185 kph). This was matched by the German *Albatros D–Va*, which could climb to 18,700 ft. (5,700 m) and reach the speed of 116 mph (187 kph). Both machines were highly maneuverable in the hands of a skillful pilot.

Zeppelins and bombers

The Germans used large airships called Zeppelins to bomb Britain. These ships scared the British. They always came at night and glided

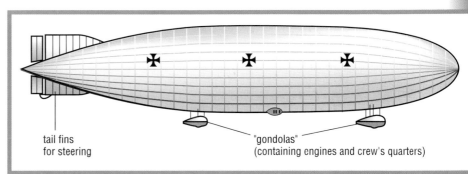

tail fins
for steering

"gondolas"
(containing engines and crew's quarters)

spookily across the sky. Streetlights were turned off and people blacked out their windows so that the Zeppelins could not see their targets. On January 19, 1915, the first Zeppelin raid on Britain took place when two Zeppelins dropped bombs on Yarmouth and King's Lynn, killing four people and injuring sixteen others. At midnight on May 31, 1915, there was a Zeppelin raid on London that killed seven people and caused widespread damage. In 1917, the Germans stopped the Zeppelin attacks and switched to using bomber aircraft. The *Gotha IV* bomber raided Britain between 1917 and 1918, causing 850 deaths. In 1918, the British began using the *Handley Page* bomber. It was capable of attacking Berlin, but the war ended before it was able to do so.

By 1916, the largest World War I German Zeppelins were almost 656 ft. (200 m) long, could carry 5 tons of bombs, and had a speed of 25 mph (40 kph).

Edward Rickenbacker—American "ace of aces"

Rickenbacker was born in Columbus, Ohio, in 1890. He first made his name as a racecar driver, and in 1911 took part in the very first Indianapolis 500. He was quick to join the army when the United States entered the war and was sent to France. There he worked on the motor-car staff of General Pershing. In March 1918, he was transferred to the Air Service. His quick reflexes made him an excellent pilot.

Rickenbacker fought 134 dogfights and had 26 "kills." On one occasion, he fought seven German planes on his own and shot down two of them. As with other air aces, he had great respect for his enemies. He once said: "Like all air fighters, I never thought of killing an individual but of shooting down an enemy plane." Rickenbacker was awarded the Congressional Medal of Honor for his bravery during World War I. He died in 1973.

Enter the United States!

When war broke out in Europe in August 1914, the United States did not take sides. Americans did not want to get involved in a war that was happening "over there," some 3,100 mi. (5,000 km) away. The United States was considered a melting pot of people from all over Europe, including Britain, Germany, and Russia. President Woodrow Wilson said that the United States had to be **neutral,** otherwise its "mixed population would wage war on each other." So why did the United States join the war in 1917?

Unrestricted submarine warfare

In May 1915, an angry President Wilson sent several messages of protest to the Germans over the sinking of the passenger ship *Lusitania*. The Germans then agreed not to attack passenger ships without first giving a warning. When unrestricted submarine warfare started again in February 1917, Germany knowingly ran the risk of war with the United States.

The Zimmerman telegram

Arthur Zimmerman was the German foreign minister. In January 1917, he sent a telegram to the German ambassador in Mexico, saying he should get the Mexican people to declare war on the United States. British agents found out about the telegram and handed a copy to the United States. It was published in U.S. newspapers on March 1, 1917. U.S. leaders were furious.

The United States declares war

In March 1917, four American ships were sunk by U-boats. This was the final straw for the United States, and President Wilson asked **Congress** to declare war on Germany. He said: "The world must be made safe for democracy. To such a task we can dedicate our lives and our fortunes, everything." On April 6, Congress voted by 531 votes to 56 to declare war on Germany. Many U.S. citizens were enthusiastic about joining the war, and flag-waving crowds paraded down Broadway in New York City.

This 1917 poster encouraged Americans to join the U.S. army. Germany is depicted as a threat to civilization (Kultur).

The American Expeditionary Force

In 1917, the United States had an army of just 250,000 men. General John Pershing was put in charge of raising a new army called the American Expeditionary Force, or AEF, that would be sent to fight in Europe. It took time to organize and train the AEF, and during 1917, only a small number of U.S. soldiers reached Europe. But by the end of the war, in November 1918, there were more than 2 million U.S. soldiers in France, including 400,000 African American soldiers.

The arrival of the AEF in Europe raised the morale of the British and French, who were near exhaustion after three years of trench warfare. It was to play an important part in the **Allied** victory on the **Western Front** in 1918.

Soldiers in the AEF were nicknamed "doughboys." It is thought the name came from the buttons on the soldiers' uniform, which looked like dumplings made of dough.

General John Joseph Pershing

Born in 1860, Pershing was nicknamed "Black Jack" because he had commanded an African American **cavalry** unit in Cuba in 1898. He suffered a great personal tragedy in 1915, when his wife and three daughters were burned to death in a fire.

Pershing was a stern man who did not tolerate incompetence, and generals who were not doing their jobs were promptly fired. The Allies wanted the U.S. troops to be under their command. But Pershing refused and insisted that the AEF be kept as a separate force under his control. After the war, he was promoted to the rank of General of the U.S. Armies. He died in 1948.

Ludendorff's Last Throw of the Dice

By early 1918, the German people were close to starvation and growing tired of the war. **Erich von Ludendorff,** the German commander, knew that it would not be long before huge numbers of U.S. troops reinforced the **Allies.** He decided to launch a series of all-out attacks on the Allied lines before the U.S. troops arrived. It was Germany's only real chance of winning the war. It was a last throw of the dice.

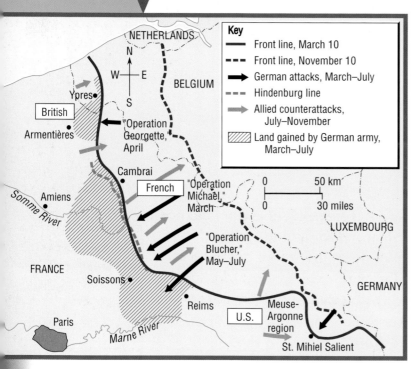

Key
— Front line, March 10
--- Front line, November 10
→ German attacks, March–July
--- Hindenburg line
→ Allied counterattacks, July–November
▨ Land gained by German army, March–July

NETHERLANDS
BELGIUM
Ypres
British
Armentières
"Operation Georgette," April
Cambrai
French
Somme River
Amiens
"Operation Michael," March
"Operation Blucher," May–July
0   50 km
0   30 miles
LUXEMBOURG
FRANCE
Soissons
GERMANY
Reims
Meuse-Argonne region
U.S.
Paris
Marne River
St. Mihiel Salient

"Operation Michael"

With Russia out of the war, the Germans were able to transfer troops from the **Eastern Front** to the west. During February and March 1918, thousands of trains carried men and equipment into northeastern France. A huge attack, code-named "Operation Michael," was to take place against the weakest part of the British lines near the Somme River.

At 4:40 A.M. on March 21, 1918, 7,000 guns opened fire on the Allied lines. In five hours, more than 1 million shells were fired, including 250,000 gas shells. The noise was deafening. After this, German troops armed with light machine guns, automatic rifles, and **flame-throwers** blazed their way through the Allied lines. In the misty conditions, there was chaos and confusion, and the Allies were pushed back. It was like a "sandcastle before an incoming tide." It was a war of movement once again. By April 5, the Germans had gained 37 mi. (60 km) of territory. However, after this success, they were unable to make any further progress.

"Operation Georgette"

On April 9, Ludendorff attacked the British lines further north near Armentières. "Operation Georgette" was intended to push the British to the English Channel. For a time, it looked like a success, and a worried General Haig sent a message to the soldiers in which he said: "Every position must be held to the last man; there must be no retirement. With our backs to the wall and believing in the justice of our cause, each one of us must fight to the end." The British put up strong resistance and, by April 29, they had blocked the German advance.

"Operation Blucher"

A third German attack took place between Soissons and Reims on May 27. The Germans once again broke through and, by July, had reached the Marne River. They were just 43 mi. (70 km) away from Paris. A huge gun, nicknamed "Long Max," was used to bombard Paris, killing 256 civilians. Eventually, the Germans were held up by a combined French–American force and pushed back across the Marne.

These German troops are climbing over a captured trench in the attack on Allied positions northwest of Soissons in June 1918.

The German army had made a great effort, but after three months of fighting, the soldiers were exhausted. An outbreak of flu in June did not help matters. The German army had advanced so far into France that it was difficult to keep it supplied. The morale of the troops began to sag and indiscipline crept into the ranks. German soldiers began looting shops, getting drunk, and criticizing their officers. By mid-July, the tide was turning against them.

A heartfelt letter

Beloved Fritz

Heartiest thanks for your dear letter. If only this cursed war would come to an end. We hope it will soon. Wilhelm Beisz was killed on June 1. A week ago the Nautmeiers received news that their son Henry had fallen and now they have had a second telegram to say that their youngest son Ludwig has been killed. What a dreadful blow to lose two sons in such a short time.

Fodder is very scarce, so much so that we can hardly feed our cattle. Tomorrow is our sad anniversary. It will be two years since our beloved and only brother was killed, and what a number have fallen in those two years. We ourselves in this small area can count 33, and yet there is no end.

With heartfelt greetings and in the hope of seeing you soon.

Your own dear and faithful
Lena

Extracts from a letter written by Lena Wieden to her soldier husband, Fritz. The letter was dated June 16, 1918. It is thought that the letter was found on his dead body.

The Allies Strike Back

From July 18, 1918, the Germans were on their heels. They began to retreat, burning down villages as they did so.

The Battle of Amiens

At 4:20 A.M. on August 8, a combined British, Australian, and Canadian force attacked the Germans near Amiens. Over 400 tanks burst through the German lines, supported by bombers and fighter aircraft. The Australians, under the command of **Sir John Monash,** advanced six miles (ten kilometers) on the first day of fighting. **Erich von Ludendorff** said it was "the black day of the German army." By August 11, the **Allies** had captured 4,000 guns and taken 30,000 prisoners. The Germans had lost the will to fight and threw down their helmets and rifles almost in relief.

Using camouflage left by the Germans who had retreated across the river, these American soldiers man the front line in the Meuse Valley north of Verdun.

The Manchester Guardian
Tuesday, July 23, 1918

GERMANS TO RETREAT AGAIN BURNING VILLAGES AND STORES

The German retreat from the Marne may extend along a line of 25 miles and to a depth of eight miles or more. The smoke of burning villages and stores has been observed behind the German lines in this region.

With the prisoners taken on Sunday and 45 guns abandoned by the Germans south of the Marne, the Allies have captured about 22,000 prisoners and 460 guns.

These places are on the map on p. 38.

The Meuse-Argonne offensive

On September 12, the American Expeditionary Force under General John Pershing pushed the Germans back in the St. Mihiel **salient,** taking 13,000 prisoners. Then, on September 26, the United States launched a big attack in the Meuse-Argonne region of eastern France. Slowly but surely, they drove the Germans back. Vital railway lines that were used to supply the German army were captured. By November, the Germans had lost all the land they had won earlier in the year. The Americans, however, paid a high price for their victory, with 26,000 dead and 97,000 wounded.

The collapse of Germany

On September 29, Allied forces broke through the **Hindenburg Line,** a heavily fortified German trench system. It was a massive blow to the Germans. The end of the war was now in sight. By November 3, Germany's allies—Bulgaria, Turkey, and Austria—had all surrendered. There was unrest in Germany, with rioting in the streets and a mutiny in the navy. On November 9, 1918, Kaiser Wilhelm II, the emperor of Germany, abdicated and fled to the Netherlands. At 5:00 A.M. on November 11, the Germans signed the **armistice** in a railway carriage at Compiègne, France. All fighting came to an end at eleven o'clock on the same morning. World War I was over.

*This cartoon appeared in the British newspaper the Daily Express on November 10, 1918. It shows Kaiser Wilhelm in a Dutch clog, or shoe. The Allies were unable to arrest him because the Netherlands was a **neutral** country.*

The beginning of the end

In early October 1918, **Ludendorff** called a meeting of his general staff to tell them that Germany had no hope of winning the war. Colonel Albrecht von Thaer later recalled the scene:

Ludendorff stood up, his face was pale and filled with deep worry but his head was still held high. He said it was his duty to tell us that our military condition was terribly serious. The war could no longer be won, but rather a defeat awaited. Soon the enemy, with the help of U.S. troops anxious to fight, would win a victory. Our army would be forced to retreat in disorder across the Rhine. Ludendorff said that he would be asking the Kaiser to seek peace by contacting President Wilson of the United States. As he spoke, quiet sobbing and moaning was audible. Many had tears running down their cheeks.

Victory, But at What Price?

News of the **armistice** was greeted with wild enthusiasm. Throughout Britain, church bells were rung and people went into the streets waving flags and setting off fireworks. The king and queen were cheered as they drove through London's Hyde Park. In Martin Place, Sydney, huge crowds burned effigies of the Kaiser and sang patriotic songs. There were joyful celebrations all over the United States. Herbert Hamm, of the Student Army Training Corps at the University of Maine, wrote: "My goodness there was an awful [large] crowd in Bangor."

Loss of life

Soon, however, the dreadful cost of the war began to sink in. More than eight million soldiers had lost their lives; more than in any other war to date. There was talk of a "lost generation" of men between the ages of 18 and 45 who had died. They certainly included many talented scientists, writers, and politicians.

Large monuments to commemorate the dead were built, as communities tried to come to terms with the loss of loved ones.

Material losses

The war left many countries in debt. The government was forced to raise taxes and increase borrowing to pay off its debts. Large areas of France and Belgium had been destroyed by artillery explosions. Forests and woodlands had been obliterated. Towns such as Ypres in Belgium had to be completely rebuilt.

The Daily Mirror reported the celebrations in London on Armistice Day in 1918.

ALLIES' DRASTIC ARMISTICE TERMS TO HUNS

The Daily Mirror
CERTIFIED CIRCULATION LARGER THAN THAT OF ANY OTHER DAILY PICTURE PAPER

No. 4,696.   TUESDAY, NOVEMBER 12, 1918.   One Penny.

HOW LONDON HAILED THE END OF WAR

Never again!

People said that such a war should never be allowed to happen again. On November 11, 1918, David Lloyd George, the British prime minister, told the House of Commons, "I hope we may say that, thus, this fateful morning, came an end to all wars." His sentiments turned out to be wishful thinking. Under the 1919 Treaty of Versailles, the **Allied** powers made Germany pay a heavy price for its part in the war. Large amounts of territory were taken from Germany and it was ordered to pay more than $32 billion. The terms of the treaty were dictated to the Germans. They were not allowed to negotiate any part of the treaty. Many Germans felt humiliated and there was a huge amount of resentment. This was one of the major reasons why, in 1939, the world was at war once again.

This huge monument is at Thiepval, near the town of Albert, on the Somme River in France. It lists the names of 73,412 soldiers who died in the Battle of the Somme and whose bodies were never found.

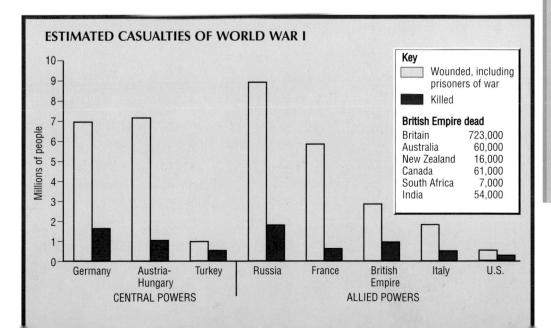

ESTIMATED CASUALTIES OF WORLD WAR I

Key
- Wounded, including prisoners of war
- Killed

British Empire dead

Britain	723,000
Australia	60,000
New Zealand	16,000
Canada	61,000
South Africa	7,000
India	54,000

Millions of people

CENTRAL POWERS: Germany, Austria-Hungary, Turkey

ALLIED POWERS: Russia, France, British Empire, Italy, U.S.

World War I Timeline

	WESTERN FRONT	EASTERN FRONT	GALLIPOLI/ MIDDLE EAST	ITALIAN FRONT AND SIDE-SHOW FRONTS	AIR AND SEA
1914	June 28: assassination of Archduke Franz Ferdinand Sept. 5–9: Battle of the Marne End of 1914: Trenches dug from English Channel to Swiss border	Aug. 26–30: Battle of Tannenberg Sept. 7–14 : Battle of the Masurian Lakes	Oct.: Turkey enters war on the side of Germany	German colonies in Africa and Pacific Ocean captured by Allies	Nov.: German ships sink two British ships at Coronel *Emden* sunk by HMAS *Sydney* Dec.: British sink German warships off the Falkland Islands
1915	April: Gas used for the first time by German army Sept.: British use gas in the Battle of Loos		April 25: First landings on Gallipoli peninsula Aug. 6: Landings at Suvla Bay Dec.: Kut besieged by Turks Evacuation of troops from Gallipoli	May: Italy enters war on side of Allies	Jan.: *Blucher* sunk by British on the Dogger Bank First Zeppelin raid on Britain Feb.: First unrestricted submarine warfare campaign May: *Lusitania* sunk
1916	Feb.: Start of the Battle of Verdun July 1–Nov. 18: Battle of the Somme Sept. 15: Tanks used for first time	June: Russian counterattack under Brusilov	April: Surrender of Kut to Turks T.E. Lawrence organizes guerrilla attacks on Turks		May 31: Battle of Jutland Zeppelin raid on London
1917	April: U.S. enters war June 7: Allies capture Messines Ridge July 31–Nov. 10: Third Battle of Ypres Nov. 6: Capture of Passchendaele Nov. 20: Battle of Cambrai	March: Czar Nicholas II abdicates Nov.: Bolsheviks seize control of Russia Dec.: Russia withdraws from the war	Dec.: Capture of Jerusalem by Allenby	Oct.–Nov.: Battle of Caporetto	Feb. 1: Germany restarts unrestricted submarine warfare April: Convoy system started Germans start using bombers to raid Britain
1918	March 21: Operation Michael Aug. 8: Battle of Amiens Sept.: Meuse-Argonne offensive Nov. 11: Armistice signed	March 3: Treaty of Brest Litovsk between Germany and Russia Nov. 3: Austria surrenders	Oct. 31: Turkey withdraws from the war	Sept.: Bulgaria withdraws from the war Oct.–Nov.: Battle of Vittorio Veneto	

Map of the World at War

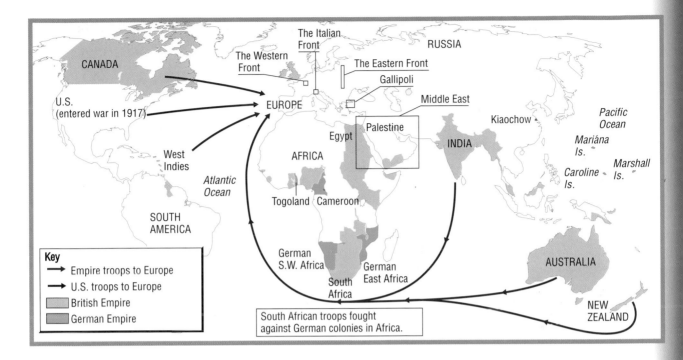

More Books to Read

Nonfiction

Banks, Arthur. *A Military Atlas of the First World War.* Conshohocken, Pa.: Cooper, Leo Books, 1997.

Gay, Kathyln and Martin K. Gay. *World War I.* Brookfield, Conn.: Twenty-First Century Books, 1995.

Hull, Robert, ed. *A Prose Anthology of the First World War.* Brookfield, Conn.: Millbrook Press, 1993.

Kent, Zachary. *World War I: "The War to End Wars."* Berkeley Heights, N.J.: Enslow Publishers, 1994.

MacDonald, John and Anthony Livesay. Introduction by Jeremy Moore. *Great Battles of World War I.* New York, N.Y.: Smithmark Publishers, 1997.

Rees, Rosemary. *The Western Front.* Chicago, Ill.: Heinemann Library, 1997.

Rice, Earle Jr. *The Battle of Belleau Wood.* San Diego, Calif.: Lucent Books, 1996.

Fiction

Bloom, Harold. *All Quiet on the Western Front.* Broomall, Pa.: Chelsea House Publishers, 2000.

Hemingway, Ernest. *For Whom the Bell Tolls.* New York, N.Y.: Simon & Schuster Trade, 1996.

Lutz, Norma Jean. *The Great War.* Uhrichsville, Ohio: Barbour Publishing, 1998.

Glossary

alliance union of countries who join together for a common purpose

Allies global term for countries united against Germany and Austria-Hungary

ANZAC short for "Australian and New Zealand Army Corps"

armistice cease-fire that precedes the signing of a peace treaty

Balkans southeastern part of Europe

battle-cruiser heavy gunned ship, smaller and faster than a battleship but made of lighter armor

bayonet long blade that can be attached to the end of a rifle

Birdwood, Sir William British-born general who was appointed to command the ANZAC forces in 1914

Bolsheviks Russian political party that followed communism. Led by Lenin, the Bolsheviks seized power in Russia during the Russian Revolution in November 1917

Brest Litovsk, Treaty of signed on March 3, 1918, between Germany and Russia, forcing Russia to pay war damages to the Germans and to give up land in Poland and the Ukraine

casualty clearing station hospital behind the front lines where wounded soldiers were taken for surgery

cavalry soldiers on horseback

colonies countries that were taken over and run by another country

Congress lawmaking group of elected officials in the United States, made up of the Senate and the House of Representatives

depth charge bomb that explodes underwater, used to sink submarines

destroyer small, fast warship

Dreadnought super battleship first built in Britain in 1906 and copied by other navies

Eastern Front important area of fighting in eastern Germany, Poland, and Galicia

empire large group of countries under the control of another country

fascine large bundle of sticks that was dropped into a trench, enabling a tank to cross

flame-thrower weapon fueled by gas or paraffin that shoots out a large flame

great powers most powerful countries in Europe in 1914, including Britain, Germany, France, Russia, Italy, and Austria-Hungary

grenade small bomb that is thrown at an enemy

guerrilla soldier who uses surprise "hit-and-run" attacks on a larger enemy force

Hindenburg Line strong defensive German trench system that ran from Arras to Laon in northeastern France

industrialized when a country's economy is based on factories that produce large amounts of goods and the majority of people live in towns and cities

infantry soldiers on foot

Kitchener, Lord British secretary of state for war in 1914, responsible for raising volunteers to fight in World War I

latrines toilets in the trenches, usually a hole in the ground containing a bucket that was emptied at night

Ludendorff, Erich von German general who planned the attack on Verdun in 1916 and the final German Spring offensive on the Allies in 1918

minefields on land, areas where explosive devices were planted in the ground. At sea, minefields were areas where mines were floated beneath the surface and detonated when the hull of a ship hit them

Monash, Sir John Australian lieutenant-general who took over for Birdwood as commander of the Australian Corps in 1918

neutral not taking sides in a war

no-man's-land area between the two opposing lines of trenches during World War I

offensive large, planned attack on an enemy

pals battalion volunteer group of men from the same town or locality

pillboxes small, concrete fortifications

Rennenkampf, Pavel Russian general who invaded East Prussia—a part of Germany—in 1914

salient bulge jutting into a line of defense or attack

Samsonov, Alexander Russian army commander who invaded East Prussia in 1914

Czar Nicholas II emperor of Russia, who was forced to give up the throne in March 1917

U-boat German submarine, short for the German word *Unterseeboot*

Western Front area of fighting during World War I made up of two parallel lines of trenches—one German and one Allied—stretching for 403 mi. (650 km) from the English Channel to the Switzerland border

Index